MW01073908

W
Jim Thorpe?

by James Buckley Jr.

illustrated by Stephen Marchesi

Penguin Workshop

For all young athletes who try
several different sports—keep it up!—JB

For my mother, Rose, and her
unwavering support and love—SM

PENGUIN WORKSHOP
An imprint of Penguin Random House LLC, New York

First published in the United States of America by Penguin Workshop,
an imprint of Penguin Random House LLC, New York, 2023

Text copyright © 2023 by James Buckley Jr.
Illustrations copyright © 2023 by Penguin Random House LLC

Penguin supports copyright. Copyright fuels creativity, encourages diverse voices,
promotes free speech, and creates a vibrant culture. Thank you for buying an authorized
edition of this book and for complying with copyright laws by not reproducing, scanning,
or distributing any part of it in any form without permission. You are supporting writers
and allowing Penguin to continue to publish books for every reader.

PENGUIN is a registered trademark and PENGUIN WORKSHOP is a trademark
of Penguin Books Ltd. WHO HQ & Design is a registered trademark
of Penguin Random House LLC.

Visit us online at penguinrandomhouse.com.

Library of Congress Cataloging-in-Publication Data is available.

Printed in the United States of America

ISBN 9780399542633 (paperback)   10 9 8 7 6 5 4 3   WOR
ISBN 9780399542640 (library binding)   10 9 8 7 6 5 4 3 2 1 WOR

Contents

Jim Thorpe and the Carlisle Indian Industrial School
football team, 1911

Who Was Jim Thorpe?

On November 11, 1911, the eleven members of the Carlisle Indian Industrial School football team ran out onto a field in Cambridge, Massachusetts. They would be playing the team from Harvard University. So far that season, Harvard had been very successful, winning five games and losing only one. They had given up only fourteen points in those six games. Harvard's was the most famous team in college football.

Carlisle was not nearly as well-known. Many fans had not even heard of the small Pennsylvania school where the students were all from Native American tribal nations. At the age of twenty-four, Jim Thorpe was Carlisle's star player and a member of the Sac and Fox Nation. He was joined by teammates who were from other tribal nations and bands, including Chippewa, Pomo, Blackfeet, and Colville. Most had grown up on reservations—areas of land created by the government to relocate Native Americans—after their ancestors had been forced to leave their homes many years earlier. Members of Harvard's team, on the other hand, were all white men who most likely came from wealthy families.

The twenty-five thousand Harvard fans in the stadium, along with football experts, figured Harvard would win easily.

Although Harvard's team was very good, it didn't have Jim Thorpe. Tall and broad-shouldered, Thorpe had powerful legs and a strong will to win. Time and again, Jim carried the ball on long runs while Harvard tried to tackle him. He used his great strength to steamroll his opponents. When he had room, he had speed to outrun them. Jim was also his team's kicker, and he made two field goals in the first half.

Meanwhile, Carlisle used plays Harvard had never seen, with the quick Carlisle players running rings around Harvard's heavier athletes. Alex Arcasa scored a touchdown for Carlisle after a long run by Jim brought the ball close to the end zone.

After three quarters, Carlisle led 15 to 9. Harvard's team was bigger and hit harder, and Carlisle's players, most of whom were smaller than Jim, were getting tired. Time was running out, and Carlisle needed another score to secure the victory.

With just a few minutes left, Jim had a chance for an important field goal—but he had a problem. He had hurt the ankle of his kicking foot a week earlier. He wore extra padding on

the ankle and taped it tightly, but it was swelling up. He wasn't sure he could make the kick— but his team needed him! "As long as I live," Jim said later, "I will never forget that moment." As the Harvard crowd screamed to distract Jim, he booted the ball forty-eight yards over the crossbar for three points. The crowd got very quiet very quickly, while Jim's teammates surrounded him, cheering.

Harvard scored once more, but it was not enough. Jim's kicks proved to be the winning points. Jim Thorpe and Carlisle had pulled off one of the biggest upsets in college sports history: Carlisle 18, Harvard 15.

"Jim . . . showed to everyone in Harvard Stadium that he had the heart of a lion," said Carlisle's coach, Glenn "Pop" Warner.

That famous game was the start of one of the greatest careers in American sports. Jim Thorpe became a two-time Olympic champion, a pro-football star, and a Major League Baseball player. He also became an inspiration and a leader for Indigenous people fighting for equality in American life. Since his glory days more than one hundred years ago, there has been no one quite like Jim Thorpe.

CHAPTER 1
Bright Path

Jim Thorpe's family tree had a lot of branches. His father, Hiram, was half Sac and Fox and half white American. In the 1800s, Hiram's Sac and Fox ancestors had been driven from their homes in the northern Midwest to small reservations in Oklahoma. Jim's mother, Charlotte, was part Potawatomi, part Kickapoo, and part French. Her ancestors, too, had been removed from their homes by the United States government to what was then called Indian Territory in Oklahoma. When Hiram and Charlotte met there in 1880, Hiram was already married and had three children. He left his other family and moved with Charlotte to a log cabin in what is now the town of Prague, east of Oklahoma City.

On May 28, 1888, Charlotte gave birth to twin boys, James (nicknamed Jim) and Charles. (Some records list their birth year as 1887. Jim himself used both dates during his life; his tomb shows 1888.) Charlotte followed Hiram's family tradition and gave the boys names in the Sac language. Charlie's Sac name is lost to history, but Jim was called *Wa-tho-Huck*, which means "path lit by a great flash of lightning." Throughout his life, Jim told people it meant "bright path." Charlotte and Hiram later had five more children, but only three of them lived to be adults.

Hiram showed his boys how to explore the wilderness that surrounded their home. He taught them to fish with a line or a spear. The boys learned to shoot rifles so they could hunt animals for the family to eat. Though Jim would become famous for his athletic ability on the sports field, he would always say that he loved fishing and hunting best.

In the years before they started school, Jim and Charlie swam in the river, sometimes building rope swings. They played lacrosse, a stick-and-ball game that had started with the Haudenosaunee (hoh-de-noh-SHOH-nee) and spread to other tribal nations. Jim also led Charlie and his

friends on long games of follow-the-leader. He
was already showing that he was the fastest and
strongest person around.

"Our lives were lived in the open, winter and
summer," Jim said. "We were never in the house
when we could be out of it."

Hiram also taught them about farming and raising cattle. The Thorpes had about four hundred cows, along with pigs and horses, on their land.

In 1887, a new US law had changed life for the Thorpes and the other Sac and Fox members. The US government passed the Dawes Act, which allowed land controlled by Indigenous people to be purchased or rented by white settlers. In Oklahoma, the Sac and Fox members would be paid for their land but not nearly as much as the land was worth. In 1891, each family in the tribal nation got only 160 acres. Everything that was left over— which was most of the tribal lands— was opened to white settlers from the East. Those settlers

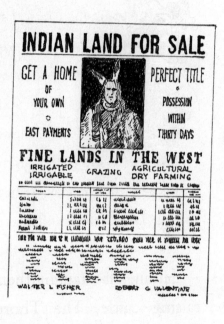

swarmed into Sac and Fox territory, creating new towns and cities almost overnight. The Thorpes rented out some of their 160 acres of land and moved to a new home on Charlotte's family's land.

Native Americans and the US Government

When Europeans arrived in the Western Hemisphere in the 1500s, they began using soldiers to force Indigenous people from their lands, allowing white settlers to move onto it.

In 1830, the United States passed the Indian Removal Act. The law allowed the government to take tribal land or force Native Americans to sell it for very little money. Sometimes, the government would sign treaties with the tribal nations to let them keep some land. However, the government often did not follow the treaties. Then, in 1851, a law called the Indian Appropriations Act forced Native Americans to move to reservations: land farther west, far away from the places where the people had lived for thousands of years. Finally, in 1887 the Dawes Act divided all land owned by tribal nations into smaller lots to be given to Native American individuals and

Native Americans forced to leave their land, 1830s

families. Many Native Americans were not able to keep or farm this land and had to move once again.

Today, there are more than 570 Tribal Nations in the United States and over 630 First Nation communities in Canada. These groups are trying to hold on to whatever land they have left and are fighting to get back some of the land that was taken from them.

For the most part, Hiram inspired Jim as the young boy grew up. Hiram excelled at anything physical, whether it was working on the farm or competing in sports and games with neighbors. However, Hiram also made life hard for Jim. He was a strong and forceful man, who often drank too much and got into fights. He sometimes used physical punishments on his boys. This led to a lot of arguments, especially between Hiram and Jim, who was much stronger than his brother. Hiram left Charlotte when Jim and Charlie were about five, though he would remain in the lives of his children even after marrying another woman.

In 1893, Jim and Charlie were sent to school. The Sac and Fox Indian Agency School was run by the Bureau of Indian Affairs (BIA), a government agency that was set up to provide services to Native Americans who were removed from their land.

Like many people and organizations of this time, the BIA believed it was the duty of white Americans to "assimilate" Native Americans. That meant to take away their identities and make them look, act, and talk like white Americans. So the students at the Sac and Fox Indian Agency School had their long hair cut and wore uniforms. They were not allowed to speak their native languages—only English. It was also a boarding

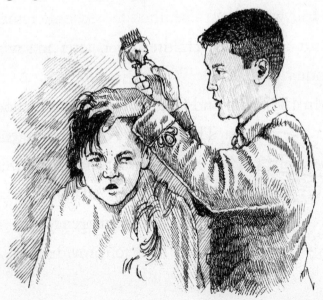

school, so students lived in dorms away from their families and traditions.

Jim did not want to be at the school. His teachers wrote that he was "uninterested in anything except the outdoor life." Soon after Hiram dropped the boys off at the school, Jim ran home. According to a family story, he used a shortcut and ran about twenty-three miles, arriving back before Hiram returned in the family's horse-drawn wagon. But Hiram made Jim return to school.

In March 1897, while at the school, Charlie became very sick. Hiram and Charlotte rushed to see him. Charlie died of pneumonia, a lung disease, at the age of eight. After losing his brother, Jim was very upset. He and Charlie had been close. Jim ran home from school yet again. He didn't want to be there without his twin. Hiram was angry. He told Jim, "I'm going to send you away so far you'll never find your way back."

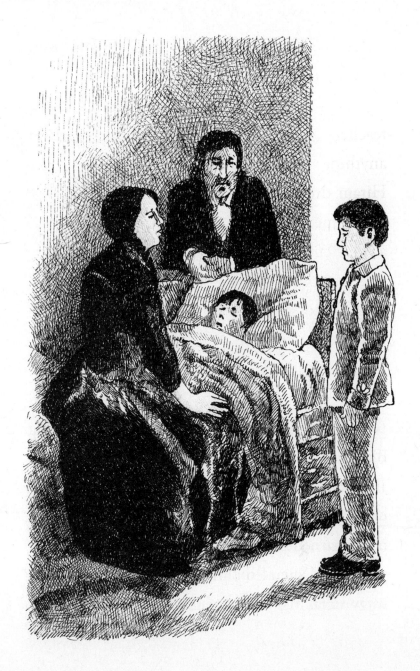

CHAPTER 2
A Star Athlete Emerges

Hiram sent Jim to the Haskell Institute, another BIA school, in Lawrence, Kansas. That was an almost three-hundred-mile train trip from Jim's home in Oklahoma. At Haskell, Jim and other boys learned skills like blacksmithing (working with metals like iron and steel), shoemaking, and wagon making. Girls learned cooking and sewing.

Jim still didn't like school and argued often with teachers about classwork. But for the first time, Jim was able to play on organized sports teams. He played football and baseball and ran track.

At Haskell, Jim also saw the mighty athletes of the Carlisle Indian Industrial School for the first time. Carlisle was another boarding school, mostly for teenagers, but some of the students

were older and took college-level classes. The Carlisle football team had come to Haskell and held a practice session. Jim looked up to these strong, proud players. "It was in Haskell [that] I saw my first football game and developed a love for it."

In summer 1901, Jim got a letter at school that said his father had been seriously injured. Once again, Jim ran away from school, this time jumping onto a train heading to Oklahoma. By the time Jim arrived, Hiram had recovered. He was very mad at Jim for leaving school again, but he let Jim remain at home. Later that year, Jim's mother, Charlotte, died after giving birth to her last child. Again, Jim decided to run away from tragedy. At only thirteen years old, he left home for Texas, where he worked on ranches training horses. Though he was still only about five feet tall, he was very strong. Jim soon became skilled at training wild horses for ranch work.

Jim returned home the next year, but Hiram continued to look for a place to send his son. He got the local BIA agent to place Jim at Carlisle in Pennsylvania in 1904.

Carlisle Indian Industrial School

Former US Army officer Richard Henry Pratt started the Carlisle Indian Industrial School in 1879 in Carlisle, Pennsylvania. It was one of the first Native American boarding schools that was fully funded by the government and was best known for its impressive athletic program and marching band. Students worked from early in the morning until dark, taking some classes in math, geography, history, and writing, but mostly learning trades like carpentry, sewing, cooking, or printing. But they were all far from their families and were treated harshly while at Carlisle.

Over ten thousand children from 140 tribal nations, such as Apache, Cherokee, Lakota, and Seneca, eventually attended Carlisle, which remained open until 1918.

Jim was at Carlisle only a brief time before news came that his father had died after being bitten by a snake. Jim was now an orphan. Although he was still close with his brothers and sisters, they lived in Oklahoma. He was so upset that he could not do his schoolwork. So the school sent him to work on a nearby farm. This was another Carlisle program, called "outings," which was created to separate the students from one another so they would become more connected to white ways of living. Jim spent most of his time until early 1907 on these outings.

One day that year, everything changed for Jim Thorpe. Now nineteen years old, Jim was back on campus, walking to meet friends, when he saw some students practicing for a track meet. They were leaping over the high-jump bar. Jim asked to try, even though he was wearing school clothes and not track gear. He easily soared over the bar that was set at five feet, nine inches high. Then he continued on to meet his friends.

The next day, Carlisle's track coach, Glenn "Pop" Warner, called Jim into his office. He told Jim he was now on the track team because his high jump had broken the school record! The meeting began a sports partnership that became world-famous.

Soon, Jim became the star of the track team, setting several more school records. In the fall, he asked to join the school's powerful and successful football team, too. Though Carlisle was not officially a college, the team's older students played against college football teams. Pop Warner, who also coached football, refused to let Jim try out. He wanted his star athlete to focus on track. But Jim came to a football practice in August 1907 and asked for a chance. Warner gave Jim a ball and told him to try to run with it. Warner expected his talented team to tackle Jim hard so that Jim would decide not to play. Instead, Jim ran, spun, leaped, and escaped all the tacklers.

Then he did it again! Warner could not keep such a talented person off the team.

Although he had played a little bit at Haskell, Jim still had a lot to learn about football at this higher level, so he spent most of the 1907 season watching and practicing. In the spring 1908 track season, Jim won hurdling events, high- and long-jump competitions, and even the hammer throw.

Glenn "Pop" Warner (1871–1954)

As a football coach for six colleges from 1895 to 1938, Glenn Warner, known as "Pop," created many of the plays, practice methods, and playing styles that were used throughout the sport until the 1940s. After coaching at the University of Georgia and Cornell University, he coached at Carlisle from 1899 to 1903 and again from 1907 to 1914. Pop Warner won national titles with his University of Pittsburgh and Stanford University teams.

When he retired in 1938, he had won more games—319 in total—than any other coach in college football. In fact, his record was not topped until 1982, when Alabama's Bear Bryant won his 320th game as a head coach. In 1934, a national youth football organization was named for him. Now known as Pop Warner Little Scholars, the organization also offers cheer and dance programs and includes 325,000 children ages five to sixteen.

After track season, he played baseball for Carlisle, too. In the fall, he returned to the football field. He was now a starting running back and the team's kicker. Jim practiced many hours to become an expert at dropkicks. Unlike today's football games, most kicks were taken without a holder. The kicker dropped the ball and struck it with his toes just as the ball landed on the ground. Jim could make field goals from more than forty yards away.

Carlisle finished that year's football season with ten wins, two losses, and a tie. Jim was named third-team All-American. That meant that football writers had voted him among the best players in the country; there were also first- and second-team All-American squads.

His 1909 track season was even better than the year earlier. At one track meet at Lafayette College, he won six different events. That spring, Jim decided he was ready to leave Carlisle and try

playing baseball in the minor leagues. This would become one of the worst decisions Jim ever made.

Minor league baseball teams played in smaller towns across the eastern and southern United States. They would look for athletes from all over and pay them to play for their teams. Jim heard about the North Carolina team, the Railroaders, from older Carlisle students and joined it.

In the fall and winter, he worked on his family's farm back in Oklahoma, where his sisters and some cousins lived. Despite the harsh treatment at Carlisle, the school had provided Jim with rules that kept his life in order. Now out of school, Jim had a tough time growing up.

Late in the summer of 1911, one of Jim's former Carlisle teammates, Albert Exendine, saw Jim in Oklahoma. He convinced Jim to return to Carlisle to rejoin the football team. Pop Warner was thrilled to have Jim back and welcomed him to the team, which had added several top players, such as Gus Welch and William Dietz.

And Jim, now twenty-three years old, was also happy. He said that it "felt good to be back among my own kind in a football uniform and on the campus of the school I loved."

Carlisle won its first eight games easily, shutting out six opponents and allowing only ten total points. In the season's sixth game, versus Pittsburgh, Jim showed off his many football talents. He ran for one touchdown and gained 235 yards running the ball. Jim was the star

runner on offense and a top tackler on defense. He was getting attention from newspapers and fans all over.

When Carlisle faced Harvard University in November of that year, they were not expected to win. Harvard had one of the best football teams in the country, and by halftime, Harvard was ahead by three points. But in the second half, Carlisle scored one touchdown, and Jim—who was playing with a hurt ankle—kicked two impressive field goals.

To most fans' surprise, Carlisle won! Jim had scored twelve of the team's eighteen points while also playing great defense. Under a headline that read "Thorpe Beat Harvard," the *Kansas City Star* newspaper called it "probably the most spectacular playing ever witnessed."

After the season, Jim was named to the All-American first team, an all-star selection and one of college football's greatest honors.

In the spring of 1912, Jim met and started dating a Carlisle student named Iva Miller.

Jim also returned to the Carlisle track team under Coach Warner. But Warner had bigger plans. He was training Jim to try for a spot on the United States Olympic team.

Iva Miller

CHAPTER 3
The 1912 Olympics

The 1912 Summer Olympics were going to take place in Stockholm, Sweden, and Pop Warner knew that Jim had a good chance to win gold. In May, Jim and Warner traveled to New York City for track meets that would determine members of the US Olympic team. Jim's two events would be the five-event pentathlon and ten-event decathlon. Those multisport competitions were perfect for Jim's many skills. In the New York City pentathlon, Jim won three events and came in second in the other two. While doing the javelin throw, he came in second even though he didn't know the proper way to hurl the spear-shaped object. Jim was so good in the pentathlon that Olympic organizers

didn't bother asking him to try out for the
decathlon—they entered him automatically!

Pentathlon and Decathlon

Groups of running, jumping, and throwing events from track and field are combined to form the multievent sports known as pentathlon and decathlon. The classic pentathlon has five events and is based on the ancient Greek Olympics. It includes the long jump, javelin throw, discus throw, 200-meter race, and 1,500-meter race. It is rarely competed anymore. The modern pentathlon has events in fencing, shooting, swimming, horse riding, and running.

Fencing

The heptathlon's 100-meter hurdles event

The decathlon, held only for male athletes, usually takes place over two days. In addition to most of the events from the classic pentathlon, the decathlon includes a high jump, pole vault, shot put, 100-meter race, 400-meter race, and 110-meter hurdles.

Female athletes take part in the seven-event heptathlon. The events are the 100-meter hurdles, high jump, shot put, 200-meter race, long jump, javelin, and 800-meter race.

In these types of competition, athletes earn points based on their results in each event. The winner is the person with the most points.

Tsökahovi "Louis"
Tewanima

Andrew Sockalexis

Howard Drew

Jim joined most of the rest of the US Olympic team on the SS *Finland* ocean liner for the journey across the Atlantic. Other Carlisle athletes were on the team, including runner Tsökahovi "Louis" Tewanima from the Hopi Nation. Carlisle's Andrew Sockalexis, a member of the Penobscot Nation, also made the team. There was only one Black athlete, sprinter Howard Drew. All the other athletes were white. Though a few female athletes were included in the 1912 Olympics, none were American. Still, US team organizers bragged about the diversity of the squad.

Before they had left, Warner had signed a form for Carlisle athletes that said none had ever competed for money. Being an amateur—which means not playing for money—was one of the most important rules of participating in the Olympics in those days.

On July 6, Jim marched with the other Americans in the Olympic opening ceremony.

Sweden's King Gustav V officially opened the games in front of a stadium full of nearly fourteen thousand fans.

The next day, Jim took part in the pentathlon. He won the long jump and came in third in the javelin. He came in first in the discus throw

and then outsprinted all the competitors to win the 200-meter dash. He won the final event, a 1,500-meter run, by more than five seconds. Jim Thorpe was now an Olympic gold medalist.

Although he was now a world champion, Jim was still the humble person he had been back at Carlisle. He didn't understand how famous he was becoming. The Swedish fans flocked to meet him when he went out between his events, and he was surprised that they knew who he was.

On July 13, the decathlon began. Normally, the event takes two days. But because so many athletes were taking part, the 1912 Olympic decathlon was held over three days. From the start, Jim showed he was the man to beat. He won the 100-meter sprint and finished third in the long jump. In the shot put, he used his great strength to make the longest throw.

Jim wears mismatched shoes during 1912 Olympics

On the morning of the second day of the events, Jim's track shoes went missing. Warner was able to find another pair, but they were not a match (Warner had even found one of them in a trash can!) and did not fit perfectly. It didn't seem to bother Jim at all. He kept up his success, winning the high jump and 110-meter hurdles.

He also finished third in the discus and fourth in the 400-meter run. Day three included a third-place finish in the pole vault and fourth place in the javelin. Jim ran the final event, the 1,500-meter run, even faster than he had in the pentathlon. He crossed the finish line with an Olympic-record time of 4 minutes, 40.1 seconds, a mark that would not be topped until 1972. His gold-medal-winning points total of 8,412.95 would not be beaten until 1932.

At the end of the games, the athletes received their awards from King Gustav V. As Jim was given his two gold medals and an oak-leaf wreath

for his head, the king said, "Sir, you are the greatest athlete in the world." Legend says that Jim answered, "Thanks, King."

After another long trip back across the ocean, Jim was honored in Pennsylvania on August 16. A large crowd at Carlisle heard speeches about Jim's accomplishments. A message from President William Howard Taft read, in part, "Your victory will serve as an incentive to all to improve those qualities which characterize the best type of American citizen." But as a member of the Sac

and Fox Nation, Jim was not recognized as a US citizen. Like other Native Americans who had spent all of their lives on American land, he would not earn citizenship until years later.

On August 24, the entire US team was treated to a parade in New York City. Jim stood by himself in the lead car and felt lonely and overwhelmed. He kept his hat on and didn't do much waving.

He said later, "I heard people yelling my name and couldn't realize how one fellow could have so many friends." Jim also added that he was more comfortable watching a parade than leading it.

Whether he liked it or not, Jim was an American hero.

CHAPTER 4
No More Medals

After all the parades were over, Jim returned to Carlisle to see his girlfriend, Iva. He also got back to playing football. Warner had again gathered a great group of players for the 1912 season. And Jim was still the big star. He led them to victory after victory against schools like Syracuse University, the University of Pittsburgh, and Lehigh University.

The next game for Carlisle was almost as big as the Harvard game in 1911. The Carlisle players would face students from the United States Military Academy, also known as Army. Newspapers at the time compared the football game to the many wars the two groups—US soldiers and Native Americans—had fought

DWIGHT EISENHOWER   OMAR BRADLEY

Army's football team, 1912

in the 1800s. As a result, Jim and his teammates
had extra reasons to put up a big win.

From the start of the game, it was clear that
Jim's team was much better than Army's. The
Carlisle players, according to Warner, "played as
one perfect, moving unit." Army did all it could
to slow Jim down. Omar Bradley, who would
later be a leading general in World War II, said,
"Thorpe runs too fast for us." In the second half,
Dwight Eisenhower and another player tried to

tackle Jim together. Instead, they whacked heads with each other and were knocked out of the game. Eisenhower later served as president of the United States from 1953 to 1961.

Carlisle won the game 27 to 6. Jim ran for almost two hundred yards, helping set his teammates up to score four touchdowns, while he kicked three extra points. The *New York Times* wrote that Thorpe "ran wild, while the Cadets

[Army players] tried in vain to stop his progress. It was like trying to clutch a shadow."

Carlisle finished the 1912 football season with twelve wins, one loss, and one tie. Jim was named All-American again. He scored twenty-seven touchdowns, more than any other player in the country, and put up 224 points for Carlisle.

A few weeks later, Jim's life changed forever. On January 22, 1913, a Massachusetts newspaper reported that Jim had once been paid to play minor league baseball. A reporter had interviewed one of Jim's old managers who had not realized that what he was telling the reporter could get Jim in trouble. The news quickly spread around the sports world.

QUESTION IS RAISED AS TO ELIGIBILITY OF JIM THORPE

SURE JIM THORPE PLAYED BASEBALL

ONLY SORROW FOR THORPE

THE SIN OF PLAYING BASEBALL ADMITTED BY THE GREAT ATHLETE.

Though Warner and others tried to fight for Jim, it was soon clear that Jim's time playing summer baseball for money meant that he was no longer an amateur. Jim didn't understand what baseball had to do with track and field. The Amateur Athletic Union (AAU) investigated. Warner wrote a letter to James Sullivan, head of the AAU, that was signed by Jim. In it, Jim apologized and said he hoped that the AAU would not judge him too harshly. But on January 27, Sullivan announced that Jim's wins would be taken out of the official record book. Jim was no longer an Olympic champion.

The public was shocked at how Jim was being treated. People from around the world wrote to the AAU demanding that Jim keep his medals.

Amateurs in the Olympics

When the modern Olympic Games began in 1896, the organizers said that athletes had to be amateurs. They could not be paid or earn money in sports.

Being an amateur athlete was not unusual at the time. In fact, being a full-time professional athlete was only just becoming possible. In the United States, baseball players and boxers were paid, but most athletes in sports like track, tennis, or golf were not. In other countries, being paid to play was even more rare. Sports such as track and field, gymnastics, or cycling were seen as part of life for wealthier people, something they did away from work.

However, the rule against professional players was lifted in the 1980s. Today, any athlete can take part in the Olympics, and most players are paid by their countries, their national Olympic organizations, or by sponsors.

Professional basketball player LeBron James plays for Team USA in the 2008 Olympics

Even his fellow competitors agreed that Jim had won fair and square. Looking back, Jim's heritage might have played a part in James Sullivan's decision. Native Americans were often treated unfairly because of their culture and the color of their skin. According to the rules, the Swedish Olympic Committee was supposed to make decisions about athletes, and the news of Jim's baseball playing had come after the deadline to

James Sullivan of the Amateur Athletic Union

make changes in the results. Still, Jim's medals were taken from him and returned to Sweden. Jim felt horrible. He told a friend at school, "I didn't have too much, and now I don't have the medals."

CHAPTER 5
Baseball and Family

Because the AAU had said he was a pro athlete, Jim could not play for Carlisle anymore, either. At twenty-five, he left Carlisle. He and Iva wanted to be married, and Jim knew he needed a job. On February 1, 1913, Jim signed

New York Giants logo

a contract to play baseball for the New York Giants in the National League (NL). The NL was part of Major League Baseball, the highest level of the sport. At the time, baseball was, along with college football, America's most popular sport. Baseball was one of the only ways for an athlete like Jim to make much money.

However, as great as Jim was on the track or the football field, he had not played baseball nearly as often or as well. It was a big jump to the major leagues from the minor league baseball he had played in North Carolina. Though Jim expected to play a lot for the Giants, they clearly signed him to attract fans who were eager to see the famous Olympian.

In March, Jim joined the Giants and their tough manager, John McGraw, for spring training in Texas. Jim worked hard to become better at batting and fielding. He was still very fast, so baserunning was his best baseball skill. There were so many reporters following Jim that he was sometimes late to practice after answering all of their questions.

Once the regular season started, though, Jim rarely played. He was sometimes a pinch hitter, taking a starter's place in the batting order. Or he was used as a pinch runner, replacing a slower

player. In all, he played only nineteen out of the Giants' 152 games in 1913.

With the money from the Giants, though,

he and Iva could settle down. They were married in Carlisle on October 14, 1913. A few days later, the couple joined the Giants on a world tour that was organized by McGraw and the Chicago White Sox owner, Charles Comiskey.

Jim marries Iva Miller, 1913

They planned to show off baseball to other countries. The tour traveled west across the United States. Huge crowds came out to watch the two teams. There were only sixteen major league teams that season, none located west of St. Louis, so seeing big stars in person attracted a lot of attention. Native Americans, especially, came to watch Jim and teammate John Meyers of the Cahuilla Nation, and they were proud to see people who looked like them playing on the field.

Jim with John Meyers

Then the group headed to Australia and Ceylon, now known as Sri Lanka. After that, they played next to the pyramids in Egypt in February.

Jim with the Giants and Chicago White Sox
at the pyramids in Egypt, 1914

Jim and Iva met Pope Pius X in Vatican City, when the teams played in Rome. The tour ended with stops in Paris and London.

In the 1914 Giants season, Jim played a little more often, appearing in thirty games. He didn't like all the time on the bench. "I feel like a sitting hen, not a ballplayer," he said.

On May 8, 1915, the couple's first child, James Jr., was born. Jim was thrilled. He missed Junior terribly when he had to leave to spend the summer on the Giants' minor league team in Jersey City, New Jersey.

Jim with his son James Jr.

In the winter, Jim was hired to help coach the football team at the University of Indiana.

In nearby Ohio, several professional teams were playing football and contacted Jim about playing for them. The Canton Bulldogs were one of these teams. Jim decided to play, and coach for them after the college season was over. His arrival was a big hit, and fans filled the stands to watch the team's games that winter. Jim also played very well. As one newspaper wrote, "by sheer strength, [he] shook off rivals like the wind blows leaves to the ground."

Playing in summer 1916 with the minor league Milwaukee Brewers, Jim had his best baseball season yet. He led the league with forty-eight stolen bases and was near the top in homers and triples. He was finally in the lineup nearly every game, many of which Iva and James Jr. came to

watch. The next year, he was in the majors again, this time with the Cincinnati Reds. He was traded back to the Giants in time to play one game in the 1917 World Series, which the Giants lost to the Chicago White Sox. Jim and Iva had their first daughter, Gail, around this time.

In September 1918, Jim's son died of a fever. Iva later said that Jim was "brokenhearted." Giants teammates said he was "never the same." Sadly, Jim began drinking because of the pain of losing his son.

Jim still had to earn a living, so he returned to baseball and football even as he dealt with his family's loss. His last major league season was with the Boston Braves in 1919. He did well, putting

up his highest batting average in the majors at .327. In the fall of 1919, Jim went back to playing professional football with the Bulldogs, and they won a league title.

Professional football was a very small sport at that time, with only a few teams and not many fans.

But it was a way for Jim to do what he loved and get paid. He led the Bulldogs to a record of nine wins and only one tie. Jim became a part owner of the team, the first Native American person to do so. Along with this big achievement, he and Iva had a second daughter, Charlotte, that same year. But Jim still felt sad about losing his son and had a difficult time connecting with people, sometimes even with his own children.

Thanks in part to Jim's fame from the Olympics, college football, and baseball, professional football began to be something people wanted to watch. His success with the Bulldogs led directly to the start of America's biggest sports league.

CHAPTER 6
Birth of the NFL

The success of professional football teams in Ohio and Pennsylvania led the team owners to form a league. On September 17, 1920, fourteen team owners met in Canton, Ohio, and voted to form the American Professional Football Association (the name was changed to the National Football League two years later). The owners wanted a popular person to be the president to help get attention for their new league. Attending the meeting as one of the owners of the Bulldogs, Jim was chosen for the job.

Jim had no idea how to run the association, and he didn't do much as president. But on the field for the Bulldogs, he played a bigger part. Even at thirty-two years old, he was still a tough man to tackle, and his skill as a kicker helped the Bulldogs have a winning season in 1920.

Jim and Iva's family was growing, too. A third daughter, Grace, was born in 1921.

That same year, Jim helped put together a football team to play in Cleveland. The team was called the Indians because along with Jim, several other former Carlisle stars played. The team only won three of its eight games. As that season ended, Jim was having a hard time. He still wanted to play baseball in the major leagues, but no team would sign him. He was not playing nearly as well, and his Indians team had done poorly. He was also drinking too much and fighting with Iva because the family had to move every time Jim found a new place to play sports.

PORTLAND, OREGON

WORCESTER, MASSACHUSETTS
HARTFORD, CONNECTICUT

In 1922, the family followed Jim to Portland, Oregon; Hartford, Connecticut; and Worcester, Massachusetts. When he did find a team to play with, Jim would be fined by them for being late or arguing with coaches.

Before the 1922 NFL season, Jim had met a man named Walter Lingo who bred a type of hunting dog called an Oorang Airedale.

Walter Lingo

Oorang Airedale

Lingo wanted to start a team named for his dogs and asked Jim to become a partner. To make their team unique, they decided to use only players from tribal nations and put on halftime performances with the dogs from Lingo's kennels. The Oorang Indians included players who were Chippewa, Mohawk, and Ho-Chunk, among others. The Oorang Indians played two seasons in the NFL but only won three games.

While with the Oorang team, Jim met a woman named Freeda Kirkpatrick and began spending time with her. In 1925, Jim and Iva divorced, and he married Freeda. In the next twelve years, the couple had four sons together: Carl Philip, William, Richard, and Jack.

Jim and Freeda with three of their sons, 1934

Jim tried to keep playing both baseball and football. But he was getting older, and it was harder for him to compete with younger players. It was so important for Jim to play sports for money that he added another activity to his busy life. He knew how to use his fame and his heritage to attract sports fans. So in the spring of 1927, he put together a team of other Native American athletes for a basketball tour. A team he called "Jim Thorpe and His World Famous Indians" played forty-five games in front of large crowds against teams in New York, Pennsylvania, and Ohio.

At the time, it was common to use the word *Indian* to describe Native American people,

and sports teams often included the word in their team names if some of their members belonged to tribal nations. But it was a misuse of the word and it is no longer acceptable to use the names of Native people for sports teams.

But after the end of his NFL career—he played one final game in 1928—Jim needed to find something else to do with his life. The league he had helped build was becoming more successful and players were making a bit more money. But Jim was considered too old to play anymore. He sometimes wished he could have made more money playing the sport he loved.

CHAPTER 7
In the Movies

By the late 1920s, Jim no longer played sports professionally, but he still wanted to find a way to stay involved. So in 1929, he took a job helping to promote a long-distance footrace.

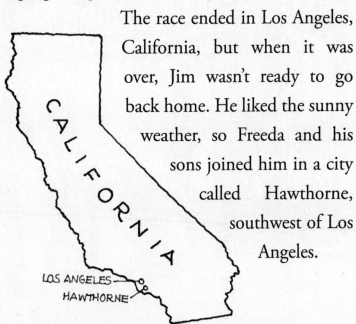

The race ended in Los Angeles, California, but when it was over, Jim wasn't ready to go back home. He liked the sunny weather, so Freeda and his sons joined him in a city called Hawthorne, southwest of Los Angeles.

By then, America was entering the Great Depression, a period of time when many companies went out of business and millions of people lost their jobs. Jim had to take whatever work he could find, including painting signs and working in construction.

Unemployed men waiting in line for free food during the Great Depression

But two things happened that gave Jim new opportunities. First, in 1929, a long article about his life was published in *Collier's* magazine. It was written by a former Olympian, Charley Paddock. The popular magazine reminded people how great Jim had been. Then, in 1932, Jim was digging ditches for a Los Angeles construction company.

Jim on a movie set, 1932

A newspaper published photos of the Olympic hero, shovel in hand. Los Angeles was home to many movie studios, and the people in charge at these studios saw a chance to take advantage of Jim's story. He was hired to act in a Western movie. Other small parts soon followed, and Jim had a new career.

That same year, the Summer Olympics were being held in Los Angeles. As a famous athlete, Jim was invited to attend some dinners and events before the games began. However, the American Olympic Committee did not give him a ticket to the actual games, as they did with other stars, all of whom were white. US vice president Charles Curtis, a member of the Kaw Nation and the first person with Native American heritage to hold that office, heard

Vice President Charles Curtis

the news about Jim being kept out and arranged for Jim to watch the games with him.

Over the next few years, Jim acted in many small roles, usually as an extra—a person in the background of scenes. Jim played a boxer, a janitor, a prison guard, a soldier, a gangster, and, not surprisingly, a football player and coach. He was often cast as a Native American person in films about Western life. In those days, the movies did not portray Native Americans accurately. Many of the roles were played by white actors wearing makeup that made their skin look darker. In the few situations where Native Americans were cast for roles, the actors were put in costumes that were not respectful to their cultures. The actors were often told to speak in grunts, and the characters they played were usually shown as impolite, unintelligent, or cruel.

In 1935, Jim set up a business to act as an agent for other Native American actors. He worked with movie studios to have correct casting, and he used his fame to protest laws that were unfair to the Native American community. He organized meetings to help people determine if the government owed them money for some of the land that was taken from them. To celebrate his heritage, he and his family performed Sac tribal dances in local shows. Jim also joined with several families in holding a large powwow in Hawthorne. A powwow is a ceremonial event in which Native Americans celebrate and pass on traditions including music, dancing, food, and more.

CHAPTER 8
Restoring a Legacy

While doing his movie work and traveling to help Native Americans, Jim left Freeda and the children alone for many weeks. And since he was no longer playing the sports he loved, he was drinking too much again. Freeda divorced Jim in 1941.

That same year, the United States entered World War II, and the whole country tried to do their part to help. At age fifty-three, Jim was too old for military service, but he worked in Dearborn, Michigan, as a guard at a factory that made machines for the army. The plant was owned by car maker Henry Ford, who hired Jim and other former athletes for these jobs, partly for their fame.

Jim had a heart attack in 1943 and was sick for weeks. He had to leave his job with Ford. After his health improved, he married again. His new wife was Patricia Askew. Jim's children were not happy about this marriage. His son William said it was "the worst thing Dad could have done." They were worried that Patricia would take advantage of Jim's fame.

Patricia Askew

After the war ended in the summer of 1945, Patricia took charge of

95

Jim's life. She worked hard to contact people who would pay him well to give speeches about sports and his life. This, along with a few acting roles, allowed Jim to make enough money to pay his bills, but he was not really happy. "Many of the things I did would have been done differently," he said later. "No one ever told me . . . no one ever guided me . . . I just did things from day to day."

In 1950, a news magazine asked nearly four hundred American sportswriters to pick the greatest athlete of the first half of the twentieth century, and they chose Jim. Newspapers around the country wrote about him, introducing many young people to him for the first time. The attention led to a movie about Jim's life. *Jim Thorpe—All-American* came out in 1951. Carlisle School showed the movie at the place where he first became a star. Jim, Patricia, and some of his children attended as special guests. As important as the occasion was, it was overwhelming for Jim, who was drinking heavily again.

In the fall of 1951, Jim was admitted into the hospital to receive treatment for mouth cancer, but he and Patricia could not pay for his operation. "We're broke," she said. Sports fans around the country were shocked, especially when they also learned he had not been paid very much for his work on the movie about his life. Several fundraising events were held, and Jim was touched by this support from his fans.

Two years later, Jim suffered another heart attack and died at the age of sixty-four.

Even though Jim Thorpe's life was over, his

story continued. Jim's children wanted to have their father buried in Oklahoma, where he was born and raised. Patricia, however, had other ideas. She learned that a pair of small towns in Pennsylvania were merging into a new, larger town in order to attract more people and businesses. The towns were called Mauch Chunk and East Mauch Chunk, and they were named for the Lenape words for "Bear Mountain" or "Bear Place." She told the town officials that if they would build a monument to Jim, and name the new town for him, she would agree to have him

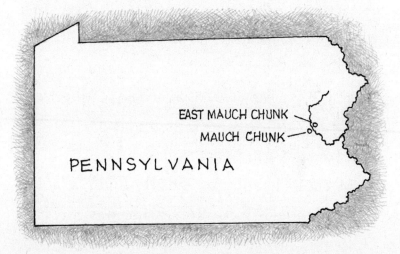

buried there, even though Jim had never been to these towns.

Both towns agreed and paid Patricia. A large tomb was built, and Jim was buried in what is now Jim Thorpe, Pennsylvania. Jim's children were very upset. They went to court to try and get their father's body back. The court cases lasted until 2015, but Jim's body remains in Pennsylvania.

Jim's tomb in Jim Thorpe, Pennsylvania

In 1963, Jim was elected as one of the first members of the Pro Football Hall of Fame. The hall honors the greatest players in NFL history. It is located in Canton, Ohio, the city where Jim and others started the NFL back in 1920.

Jim was in the news again in 1983. His family had worked for years to have his Olympic medals returned. Time after time, the leaders of the International Olympic Committee (IOC) had refused. Finally, a new IOC president, Juan Antonio Samaranch, changed the ruling.

The Pro Football Hall of Fame

Because Canton, Ohio, played such a big part in the early history of the NFL, its residents started the call for a building to honor the game's greats.

The Pro Football Hall of Fame opened in 1963 in a building topped with a football-shaped dome. Jim Thorpe was one of eleven players in the first annual class elected by the hall of fame's voters. Since then, new members are added each year, chosen by a Hall of Fame committee made up of football writers and other experts. Through 2022, there were 362 players enshrined in the hall. Each is honored with a bronze bust. Other contributors to football history are elected, including team owners, officials, and coaches.

As a museum about the history of pro football, the hall of fame is also a popular tourist attraction, drawing two hundred thousand visitors each year. Many come to the summer ceremony during which new members are welcomed to the hall.

Jim's children accepting his replacement
Olympic medals from the IOC, 1983

A ceremony was held in Los Angeles, and Jim's children were given replacement medals for the ones taken from him. In 2022, the IOC made Jim the sole champion of the two events, and they announced their decision on the 110th anniversary of Jim receiving his Olympic gold medals.

In 2000, a news magazine asked American sportswriters to vote again, this time about events from the entire twentieth century. Though many decades had passed since Jim's time on the field, his achievements were still ranked among the best. The US Congress made their own award and named Jim its number one athlete of the century. Although he had to overcome a few hurdles in his personal life, Jim Thorpe kept fighting to be a champion, on and off the field.

Timeline of Jim Thorpe's Life

1888	Jim Thorpe is born on May 28 in Oklahoma
1897	Twin brother, Charlie, dies at age eight
1904	Begins attending Carlisle Indian Industrial School in Pennsylvania
1911	Named All-American in college football
1912	Wins gold medals in pentathlon and decathlon at the Summer Olympics in Stockholm, Sweden
1913	Olympic medals taken away after it is revealed he was paid to play baseball
	Joins the New York Giants baseball team
	Marries Iva Miller
1918	Son, James Jr., dies at age three
1920	Named president of new pro football group (later called the National Football League)
1925	Marries second wife, Freeda Kirkpatrick
1929	Moves to Los Angeles and later begins working in movies
1945	Marries third wife, Patricia Askew
1953	Dies in Los Angeles at the age of sixty-four
1963	Elected to the first class of the Pro Football Hall of Fame
1983	His gold medals are returned to his family by International Olympic Committee

Timeline of the World

1865 — Civil War ends in the United States

1898 — The Spanish-American War ends

1903 — Wright brothers fly the first successful self-powered airplane at Kitty Hawk, North Carolina

1911 — Marie Curie, the first woman to win a Nobel Prize, is awarded the Nobel Prize in Chemistry (she also won the Nobel Prize in Physics in 1903 with her husband)

1918 — The influenza pandemic begins

1922 — Ireland becomes an independent country, separating from Great Britain

1927 — Philo Farnsworth helps invent television

1929 — Stock market crash begins the Great Depression

1932 — The Summer Olympics are held in Los Angeles, California

1945 — World War II ends

1947 — Jackie Robinson becomes first Black player in Major League Baseball in the twentieth century

1958 — The Baltimore Colts win the NFL championship in overtime in the first nationally televised NFL championship game

1990 — Congress passes new laws that protect Native American languages and calls for the return of artifacts to tribal nations

Bibliography

*Books for young readers

Buford, Kate. *Native American Son: The Life and Sporting Legend of Jim Thorpe*. New York: Alfred A. Knopf, 2010.

Jenkins, Sally. *The Real All Americans: The Team That Changed a Game, a People, a Nation*. New York: Doubleday, 2007.

*Labrecque, Ellen C. *Jim Thorpe: An Athlete for the Ages*. New York: Sterling, 2010.

*Long, Barbara. *Jim Thorpe: Legendary Athlete*. Springfield, NJ: Enslow Publishing, 1997.

*Sheinkin, Steve. *Undefeated: Jim Thorpe and the Carlisle Indian School Football Team*. New York: Roaring Brook, 2017.